With Love,

Trez Ibrahim

For The Love Of Teaching

Inspirational quotes for a teacher's spirit, strength and sanity.

Trez Ibrahim

Silver Laurel Publishing House
Tustin, California

SILVER LAUREL
PUBLISHING HOUSE

www.silverlaurelpublishing.com

Trez Ibrahim
Silver Laurel Publishing House
360 East First St., #426
Tustin, CA 92780
800-249-8131
info@apluseducationconsulting.com
www.APlusEducationConsulting.com
www.SilverLaurelPublishing.com

Warning – Disclaimer

iv

Dedication

This book is dedicated to my beautiful, amazing son, Brandon Brown, the love of my life. Every day I walked into my classroom, I asked myself, what would I love my son's experience in his own classroom to be like. I taught my students the way I wanted you to be taught and I worked at being the best teacher a mother would want for her child.

Brandon, you have been my greatest love, my light and my inspiration to be the best mother, teacher and woman I could be. I love you more than you'll ever know.

Praise For
The Love of Teaching

For the Love of Teaching provides such daily motivation and inspiration! Every teacher should have these on their desk and use it to stay fueled to make a positive difference!

Travis Brown
Educational Consultant & Keynote Speaker

Motivation is like food, you need to get some everyday. Anyone can teach, but the best teachers possess an immeasurable well of inspiration, insight, patience and love for their students. Trez Ibrahim journeys into what separates world-class teachers from the merely good teacher; those who continue to inspire long after they have touched a life.

Forbes Riley
CEO SpinGym & TV Celebrity Host

This one set of quotations, compiled from multiple sources and time periods, is a must for every student and teacher you know. Fun, profound and thought provoking; you'll find it hard to put it aside once you start using it.

James Malinchak
Featured on ABCs Hit TV Show,
"Secret Millionaire", Co-Author,
Chicken Soup for the College Soul,
Founder, Millionairefreebook.com

Motivation, stimulation and inventive brilliance, all neatly packaged in a small book of great little quotes from some of the best thinkers of past and present. It is a must read for all teachers and educators: for K-12 and higher education alike!

Professor Jerome Vincent Carter
Loyola Marymount
www.Inspiration52.com

A triumphant book which will make you smile, lift your soul and keep you going when life throws those little curve balls at you.

Kevin Harrington
CEO Kevin Harrington Enterprises
Original Shark from Shark Tank

A unique and inspiring book of quotes which will raise your spirits when you need it most.
Dr. Danny Brassell
Internationally-Acclaimed Speaker & Best Selling Author of "Bringing Joy Back Into The Classroom." (www.DannyBrassell.com)

Trez Ibrahim has been a friend for years. She's smart, dedicated, has a huge heart and is committed to working with people of all ages to create positive, extraordinary, lasting change. I highly recommend any material from Trez that you can get your hands on.

Ruben Mata
International Speaker, Trainer, Author

Contents

Foreword

I have had the privilege of working with and reaching millions of people over the last 40 years helping them to live the life of their dreams and one thing I've learned is that being successful in life requires positive focus. It means hanging in there and persisting, even when it sometimes seem easier to just give up. It is of crucial importance to remain confident in your abilities, confident in your desires and confident in your future, rather than to dwell on any past failure. This is exactly what successful people do.

But where do we learn how to persist, to believe in ourselves and to continue to strive for what we desire in life? Children, with their sponge-like brains and hearts, soak up the world around them. The knowledge, attitudes, and beliefs of their family, friends and teachers can affect the rest of their lives. They learn and achieve through mistakes and disappointments as well as triumphs and successes. Those around them become their mirror reminding them how valuable and precious they are as human beings.

Children spend the majority of their childhood in a classroom, learning from their teachers, directly and indirectly, how to believe in themselves and persevere through life. They grow into fruitful adults by learning those lessons and being inspired by their teachers. One can never know how far that touch will reach. As Henry Adams once said, *"A teacher affects eternity; he can never tell where his influence stops."*

In life, we have all been teachers and we have all been students. Whether you have taught a child, a friend, a mentee or a client, you have bestowed upon them your wisdom, your confidence, your belief in their power and ability to succeed and have been by their side through their successes and their failures.

This wonderful book is full of inspirational quotes that will move a teacher, coach or mentor to be the best he or she can be, to offer guidance during those inevitable tough times in life and to inspire others to stretch beyond their wildest dreams. Of course Trez added a little humor, just because in life we all need to laugh. "For the Love of Teaching" is for teachers and their students to share, to be inspired and to enjoy. Allow what you see on these pages to permeate your life and your vocation. May you continue to be the light to shine the greatness within each and every life you touch.

I hope you enjoy it, and get as much from it as I know you can.

Jack Canfield
Co-creator, #1 New York Times best selling series *Chicken Soup for the Soul*®
Author, *The Success Principles*
www.jackcanfield.com

Acknowledgements

No project ever comes to fruition without the guidance, love and support of the people around you; the people that believe in you, the ones that cheer you on and the ones that provide the emotional and logistical support and guidance that make the earth move. I have had many such people in my life. My only fear is leaving out those who have had an impact on my life and supported me on my journey to living the best life I can live.

My greatest love and gratitude go to my parents, Safwat and Afaf Ibrahim, who left this earth plane at such a young age but who have left an indelible mark on my heart and a desire and drive to live my dreams, love my life and share kindness everywhere I go. Their unconditional love towards me is something I strive to emulate every day. Mom and dad, I know you are in heaven and have been watching me grow and I pray that you are proud of the woman you have guided me to become.

To my chosen sisters, Angela and Helen. I love you both so much. I don't know how I could have made the last 40 years without you both by my side. Thank you for the friendship, the love, the laughter, and the wonderful adventures. I look forward to the next 40 years with you and many more wonderful escapades.

Thank you to my mentors, teachers, coaches and guides who have supported me, taught me, and challenged me to grow. Mary Morrissey, Jack Canfield, Deepak Chopra, Marianne Williamson, Michael Stevenson, James Malinchak, Danise Jarrett, Brodie Whitney, Ruben Mata, Dan Plum, Virginia Chavez, Wayne Dyer, Cheryl Richardson, Anthony Robbins, Louise Hay, Mark Victor Hansen, Michael Bernard Beckwith, Bob Proctor, James Van Praagh, Sonia Choquette, Rhonda Britten, Agapi Stasinopolous, Brian Tracy, Brendon Burchard, T Harv Ecker, Chris Howard, John Gray, Jean Houston, Debbie Ford, and Collin Powell.

I want to thank my colleagues and partners in education who have inspired me to grow and learn and have shown me how to connect with my students to make the greatest impact every single day. Gwen, Merrie Lynn, Sheryal, Barbara and Shawn, thank you for your support and guidance when I needed the push to keep going. Rory, Janice, Sarah and Tonia, for demonstrating to me what exemplary teaching looks like and for Trinita, for being my rock in the classroom.

Of course, I want to thank all my students. Thank you for showing me that you can break through all the challenges and adversities life throws your way. Thank you for loving me and allowing me to love you, for stretching me and allowing me to be part of your life and for bringing fun and laughter to my days.

For those I've left out, please know that you are appreciated and loved and I am truly grateful for you in my life!

With heartfelt love and gratitude,

Trez Ibrahim

Introduction

Teachers have one of the most important jobs in the world. When teachers are shaping young hearts and minds, they are literally shaping the future of our planet. Behind every successful person and story is a series of teachers – of educators, mentors, and coaches, those who helped that individual rise to distinction, ascend to a prominent place in society and make a difference in the world.

The opportunity to nurture young minds and help them transform into the leaders of tomorrow is an honor, a gift and a calling. A teacher is never just a teacher. A teacher often has to play the role of mom, dad, nurse, counselor, advisor, lawyer, judge and jury. Great teachers inspire possibilities; have an intuitive spirit and a propensity for learning. On a daily basis, they strive to teach students to display kindness, compassion, integrity, trust and respect, and they believe true teaching is reciprocal.

I fell in love with teaching from the moment I stepped foot in the classroom. I loved working with young active students and treasured observing their transformation from thinking they "can't", to realizing they can!!! My students have inspired me, motivated me and taught me many lessons about life, possibility and the resilient human spirit.

At some point in our lives, everyone becomes a teacher in some way shape or form. In this book, I've compiled some of my favorite quotes that have kept me and my students inspired and on track throughout the years. And, since there are times life can get a little crazy, I've added some comic relief, just to keep things in perspective. My hope is that this little book of quotes will remind you of the value you bring to every child you come across, to inspire you to dream big, and to believe in yourself. I hope to inspire you to honor those who have made a difference in your life, to engage each and every person you meet on the highest level, and continue to pay it forward.

This book makes a great gift for that special teacher, mentor or coach in your life or for someone who aspires to be one. Enjoy this collection and I would love to hear from you. Please share your experiences in learning and teaching, how you have used these quotes and any stories you would love to share. Feel free to email me at

info@APlusEducationConsulting.com

What Is A teacher?

A teacher is someone who sees each child as a unique person and encourages individual talents and strengths.

A teacher looks beyond each child's face and sees inside their souls.

A teacher is someone with a special touch and a ready smile who takes the time to listen to both sides and always tries to be fair.

A teacher has a caring heart that
respects and understands.

A teacher is someone who can
look past disruption and rebellion,
and recognize hurt and pain.

A teacher teaches the entire
child and helps to build
confidence and raise self-esteem.

A teacher makes a difference in
each child's life and affects each
family and the future of us all.

~ Barbara Cage

A Teacher's Gift

A teacher is a very special person who uses his or her creativity and loving, inquiring mind to develop the rare talent of encouraging others to think, to dream, to learn, to try, to do!

~ Beverly Conklin

*T*o the world you may just be a teacher, but to your students you are a HERO.

~Anonymous

A teacher affects eternity; he can never tell where his influence stops.

~ Henry Adams

It is the supreme art of the teacher to awaken joy in creative expression and knowledge.

~ Albert Einstein

What sculpture is to a block of marble, education is to a human soul.

~ Joseph Addison

To believe that a great teacher is a great artist and that there are as few as there are any other great artists. Teaching might even be the greatest of the arts since the medium is the human mind and spirit.

~ John Steinbeck

Every child deserves a champion – an adult who will never give up on them, who understands the power of connection and insists that they become the best that they can possibly be.

~ Rita Pierson

A good teacher can inspire hope, ignite the imagination, and instill a love of learning.

~ Brad Henry

*T*eaching children is an accomplishment; getting children excited about learning is an achievement.

~ Robert John Meehan

The teacher, if indeed wise, does not bid you to enter the house of their wisdom, but leads you to the threshold of your own mind.

~ Kahlil Gibran

The hardest thing to teach is how to care.

~Anonymous

A good teacher is like a candle – it consumes itself to light the way for others.

~ Mustafa Kemal Atatürk

$\mathcal{Y}$ou can teach a student a lesson for a day; but if you can teach him to learn by creating curiosity he will continue the learning process as long as he lives.

~ Clay P. Bedford

$\mathcal{I}$t takes a big heart
to help shape little
minds.

~ Anonymous

$\mathcal{A}$ teacher takes a
hand, opens the mind
and touches the heart.

~ Author unknown

The best teachers
teach from the heart,
not from the book.

~ Anonymous

Education is not the
filling a pail, but the
lighting of a fire.

~ William Butler Yeats

*I*deal teachers are those who use themselves as bridges over which they invite their students to cross, then having facilitated their crossing, joyfully collapse, encouraging them to create bridges of their own.

~ Nikos Kazantzakis

I like a teacher who gives you something to take home to think about besides homework.

~ Lily Tomlin

*O*ne child, one teacher, one book, one pen can change the world.

~ Malala Yousafzai

*T*eaching is not a lost art, but the regard for it is a lost tradition.

~ Jacques Barzun

Teachers are like
flowers: they spread
their beauty throughout
the world. Their love of
learning touches the
hearts of their students,
who then carry that
sense of wonder with
them wherever they may
go. Teachers, with their
words of wisdom, awaken
the spirit within us all
and lead us down the
roads of life.

~ Deanna Beisser

God Bless The Teacher

God bless the
teacher...For in your
care each day, you
teach the children to
laugh and play and enjoy
their lives that are still
unspoiled by a world
that is sometimes hard
to understand.

God bless the teacher...
You build your students'
hopes and dreams and
self-esteem. You teach

them compassion,
friendship, and loyalty.

You help them grow and
teach them things that
matter most. You teach
them how to be
themselves.

God bless the teacher...
For being there to calm
your students' fears,
cheer them up, and dry
their tears.

Thank you for
everything you do.

~ Julia Escobar

For The Love Of Learning

*I*magination is more important than knowledge.

~ Albert Einstein

*T*he only source of knowledge is experience.

~ Albert Einstein

Education breeds confidence. Confidence breeds hope. Hope breeds peace.

~ Confucius

Education is not preparation for life; education is life itself.

~ John Dewey

A mind when stretched by a new idea never regains its original dimensions.

~ Anonymous

Children must be taught how to think, not what to think.

~ Margaret Mead

$\mathcal{L}$earning is never cumulative, it is a movement of knowing which has no beginning and no end.

~ Bruce Lee

$\mathcal{W}$hat we learn with pleasure we never forget.

~ Alfred Mercier

Education is what survives when what has been learned has been forgotten.

~ B.F. Skinner

Logic will get you from A to B. Imagination will take you everywhere.

~ Albert Einstein

Not having heard
something is not as good
as having heard it;
having heard it is not as
good as having seen it;
having seen it is not as
good as knowing it;
knowing it is not as good
as putting it into
practice.

~ Xun Kuang, a Chinese
Confucian philosopher

*T*ell me and I forget.
Teach me and I
remember. Involve me
and I learn.

~ Benjamin Franklin

Every Teacher Has A Story

I cannot teach anybody anything, I can only make them think.

~ Socrates

I am not a teacher, but an awakener.

~ Robert Frost

*T*eaching is a process of becoming that continues throughout life, never completely achieved, never completely denied. This is the challenge and the fun of being a teacher – there is no ultimate end to the process.

~ Frances Mayforth

If you are planning for a year, sow rice; if you are planning for a decade, plant trees; if you are planning for a lifetime, educate people.

~ Chinese Proverb

I praise loudly; I blame softly.

~ Catherine II (The Great)

$\mathcal{T}$he best thing about being a teacher is that it matters. The hardest thing about being a teacher is that it matters every day.

~ Todd Whitaker

$\mathcal{N}$othing liberates our greatness like the desire to help, the desire to serve.

~ Marianne Williamson

You really *can* change the world if you care enough.

~ Marian Wright Edelman

I never teach my pupils, I only provide the conditions in which they learn".

~ Albert Einstein

Only the brave should teach. Only those who love the young should teach. Teaching is a vocation. It is as sacred as priesthood; as innate a desire, as inescapable as the genius which compels a great artist. If he has not the concern for humanity, the love of living creatures, the vision of the priest and the artist, he must not teach.

~ Pearl S. Buck

If you have
knowledge, let others
light their candles at it.

~ Margaret Fuller

If shouldn't matter
how slowly some
children learn as long as
we are encouraging
them not to stop.

~ Robert John Meehan

*T*he greatest sign of success for teacher... Is to be able to say, "The children are now working as if I did not exist".

~ Maria Montessori

*W*e never know which lives we influence, or when, or why.

~ Stephen King

The function of education is to teach one to think intensively and to think critically. Intelligence plus character – that is the goal of true education.

~ Martin Luther King, Jr.

I've come to a

frightening conclusion that I am the decisive element in the classroom. It's my personal approach that creates the climate. It's my daily mood that makes the weather. As a teacher, I possess a tremendous power to make a child's life miserable or joyous. I can be a tool of torture or an instrument of inspiration.

I can humiliate or heal. In all situations, it is my response that decides whether a crisis will be escalated or de-escalated and a child humanized or dehumanized.

~ Haim G. Ginott

$\mathscr{P}$art of teaching is helping students learn how to tolerate ambiguity, consider possibilities, and ask questions that are unanswerable.

~ Sara Lawrence Lightfoot

For That Gentle Nudge

One looks back with appreciation to the brilliant teachers, but with gratitude to those who touched our human feelings. The curriculum is so much necessary raw material, but warmth is the vital element for the growing plant and for the soul of the child.

~ Carl Gustav Jung

If you want to build a ship, don't drum up people together to collect wood and don't assign them tasks and work, but rather teach them to long for the endless immensity of the sea."

~ Antoine de Saint-Exupéry

*S*eek opportunities to show you care. The smallest gestures often make the biggest difference.

~ John Wooden

*W*e can teach from our experience, but we cannot teach experience.

~ Sasha Azevedo

*T*reat people as if they were what they ought to be and you help them become what they are capable of becoming.

~ Goethe

*T*eachers should guide without dictating, and participate without dominating.

~ C.B. Neblette

The dedicated life is
the life worth living.
You must give with your
whole heart.

~ Annie Dillard

There is no such
whetstone, to sharpen a
good wit and encourage
a will to learning, as is
praise.

~ Roger Ascham

*D*on't just teach your kids to read, teach them to question what they read. Teach them to question everything!

~ George Carlin

*D*o not confine your children to your own learning, for they were born in another time.

~ Chinese Proverb

You can't direct the
wind but you can adjust
the sails.

~ Anonymous

The art of teaching is
the art of assisting
discovery.

~ Mark van Doren

*W*isdom cannot be imparted. Wisdom that a wise man attempts to impart always sounds like foolishness to someone else ... Knowledge can be communicated, but not wisdom. One can find it, live it, do wonders through it, but one cannot communicate and teach it.

~ Hermann Hesse, Siddhartha

$\mathcal{E}$verybody is a genius, but if you judge a fish by its ability to climb a tree, it will live its whole life believing that it is stupid.

~ Albert Einstein

$\mathcal{K}$ids don't care how much you know until they know how much you care.

~ Dr. Madeline Hunter

Teachers At Heart

*B*ecome a possibilitarian. No matter how dark things seem to be or actually are, raise your sights and see the possibilities – always see them, for they're always there.

~ Norman Vincent Peale

There is a vitality, a
life force, an energy, a
quickening that is
translated through you
into action, and because
there is only one of you
in all of time, this
expression is unique.
And if you block it, it
will never exist through
any other medium and it
will be lost. The world
will not have it. It is not
your business to
determine how good it is
nor how valuable nor

how it compares with other expressions. It is your business to keep it yours clearly and directly, to keep the channels open.

~ Martha Graham

And whatsoever ye do, do it heartily.

~ Colossians 3:23

The cards you hold in the game of life mean very little – it's the way you play them that counts.

~ West African saying

When the whisper comes to do something really spectacular, most people are consumed by the fear of leaving their Comfort Zones... Follow your bliss. Chase rainbows.
Do the unthinkable.
Your dream life is waiting for you.

~ Michael Stevenson

*L*ove is a choice, it's a decision you make to wake up every morning and choose to love the person you are with more each day.

~ Afaf Ibrahim (my mom)

*W*e don't know who we are until we see what we can do.

~ Martha Grimes

*L*iving at risk is
jumping off the cliff
and building your wings
on the way down.

~ Ray Bradbury

*T*here are two ways of
meeting difficulties: you
alter the difficulties or
you alter your self to
meet them.

~ Phyllis Bottome

Whatever you can do
or dream you can, begin
it. Boldness has genius,
power and magic in it.
Begin it now.

~ Goethe

When everybody tells you that you are being idealistic or impractical, consider the possibility that everybody could be wrong about what is right for you. Look inside yourself the way nobody else can... How much better to know that we have dared to live our dreams than to live our lives in the lethargy of regret.

~ Gilbert E Kaplan

For Your Students

*B*etter to strive and climb, and never reach your goal, than to drift along with time – an aimless, worthless soul, Ay, better to climb and fall, or sow, though the yield be small, than to throw away day after day, and never strive at all.

~ Grace B Hinkey

*O*ur deepest fear is not that we are inadequate. Our deepest fear is that we are powerful beyond measure. It is our light, not our darkness that most frightens us. We ask ourselves, who am I to be brilliant, gorgeous, talented, fabulous? Actually, who are you *not* to be? You are a child of God. Your playing small does not serve the world. There is nothing enlightened about shrinking so that other people won't feel insecure around you. We are all meant to shine, as children do. We were born to make manifest the glory of God that is within us. It's not just in some of us; it is in everyone. And as we let our own light shine, we unconsciously give other people permission to do the same. As we are liberated from our own fear, our presence automatically liberates others.

~ Marianne Williamson

To do something better, you must work an extra bit harder.... Any job one takes on must be grasped and felt with one's soul, mind and heart.

~ Mikhail Gorbachev

We must dare, and dare again, and go on daring.

~ Georges Jacques Danton

Yesterday I dared to struggle. Today I dare to win.

~ Bernadette Devlin

I can't imagine a person becoming a success who doesn't give this game of life everything he's got.

~ Walter Cronkite

Build your self-
esteem by recalling all
the ways you have
succeeded, and your
brain will be filled with
images of you making
your achievements
happen again and again.
Give yourself permission
to toot your own horn,
and don't wait for
anyone to praise you.

~ Jack Canfield

Cultivate your garden... Do not depend upon teachers to educate you... Follow your own band, pursue your curiosity bravely, express yourself, make your own harmony... In the end, education, like happiness, is individual, and must come to us from life and from ourselves.

~ Will Durrant

When you see the word 'impossible', you should always see "I'm Possible!"

~James Malinchak

Do not follow where the path may lead. Go instead where there is no path and leave a trail.

~ Muriel Strode

Don't give up. Keep going. There is always a chance that you will stumble onto something terrific. I have never heard of anyone stumbling over anything while he was sitting down.

~ Ann Landers

You do what you can for as long as you can, and when you finally can't, you do the next best thing.... But you don't give up.

~ Charles "Chuck" Yeager

Don't wait for your ship to come; swim out to it.

~ Steve Southerland

You will never be more ready to achieve your dreams than right now, because your most important resource is time. It's the only thing you cannot get back.

~ Michael Stevenson

Struggle and survival, losing and winning, doesn't matter. It's entering the race that counts. You enter, you can win, you can lose... but it's all about entering the race.

~ Pam Grier

$\mathcal{K}$eep in mind that part of growing up is dealing with difficult issues, and the benefits can be great if you have the courage to ask for help. Human beings are not designed to go through life alone. No one has to bear the burden of tough times all by themselves.

~ Jack Canfield

It was a high counsel that I once heard given to a young person, "Always do what you are afraid to do."

~ Ralph Waldo Emerson

I am a great believer in luck, and I find the harder I work the more I have of it.

~ Stephen Butler Leacock

If you think you can
or you think you can't,
you're right.

~ Henry Ford

When you knock on
the door of opportunity,
it's work that answers.

~ Brendon Burchard

Everything you want
is on the other side of
your comfort zone.

~Jack Canfield

Reach for the stars,
the worst you can do is
land on the moon.

~ Safwat Ibrahim (my dad)

*D*on't wait for
something big to occur.
Start where you are,
with what you have, and
that will always lead you
into something greater.

~Mary Morrissey

When All Else Fails, Lower Your Expectations

*D*ear parents, if you promise not to believe everything your child says happens at school, I'll promise not to believe everything he says happens at home.

~ Friars Club

For every person who wants to teach there are approximately thirty people who don't want to learn much.

~ W.C. Stellar

Keep calm and pretend this is on the lesson plan.

~ Keep calm studio

*T*eaching: 65 hours per week for 36 weeks equals 2340 work hours. Other jobs: 40 hours per week for 52 weeks equals 2080 work hours. So I deserve the summer off. Any other questions?

~ Author unknown

*T*eacher: where is your homework? Me: I lost it fighting this kid who said you were the worst teacher in school.

~ Author unknown

*O*nce you master the art of facing a room full of teenagers, and come out of live, you can do anything.

~ Chasing Pegasus

If you ever want to know what a teacher's mind field looks like, imagine a web browser with 2879 tabs open. All. The. Time.

~ Author unknown

If you didn't get the grade you wanted, it's highly possible I didn't get the work I wanted.

~ Author unknown

Oh you don't understand? Let me explain again the exact same way.

~ Unhelpful school teacher

Teacher: Why are you talking during my lesson? Student: Why are you teaching during my conversation?

~ Author unknown

My teacher pointed at me with this ruler and said "At the end of this ruler, there is an idiot!" I got detention after asking which end.

~ Author unknown

I do this for the money, said no teacher ever.

~ Author unknown

Anyone who can only think of one way to spell a word obviously lacks imagination.

~ Mark Twain

I will not yell in class. I will not throw things in class. I will not have a temper tantrum. I will always be good. Because I am the teacher. I'm the teacher. I'm the teacher...

~ Author unknown

Early one morning, a mother went in to wake up her son.

"Wake up, son. It's time to go to school"

With the covers pulled over his head, he replied, "but why, Mom? I don't want to go to school."

"Give me two reasons why you don't want to go" she asked.

"Well, the kids hate me

for one, and the teachers hate me, too!"

"Oh, that's no reason not to go to school. Come on now and get ready."

"Give me two reasons why I should go to school" he responded.

"Well, for one, you're 52 years old. And for another, you're the Principal!"

~ Author unknown

Why God made teachers

When God created teachers, he gave us special friends to help us understand his world and truly comprehend the beauty and the wonder of everything we see, and become a better person with each discovery.

When God created teachers, he gave a special guides to show

us ways in which to grow so we can all decide how to live and how to do what's right instead of wrong, to lead us so that we can lead and learn how to be strong.

Why God created teachers, in his wisdom and his grace, was to help us learn to make our world a better, wiser place.

~ Kevin William Huff

About the Author

Trez Ibrahim is a consultant, speaker, trainer, author and Founder/CEO of A+ Education Consulting and Life Mastery Solution. She is a National Board Certified Educator, holds a Master's Degree in Education, and has been responsible for numerous leadership and training roles within the school district including Special Education, Master Teacher, Female Leadership Academy and Professional Development trainings. She has been teaching for over 15 years and is dedicated to building real connection with students so that they can get in touch with their highest potential and learn to be powerful, happy and successful citizens of the planet. She also dedicates her time in helping educators become successful through motivation, inspiration and a common-sense approach to teaching and classroom management.

She is available to speak with your group and can be reached at info@ apluseducationconsulting.com

www.ingramcontent.com/pod-product-compliance
Lightning Source LLC
Chambersburg PA
CBHW021239090426
42740CB00006B/613